POETRY AND THE CONCEPT OF MAYA

Poetry and the Concept of Maya

A Textbook for Poets

BASED ON THE POETRY OF
Alan Britt

TEXT AND COMMENTARY BY
David Churchill

Pony One Dog Press
Washington, DC

Poetry and the Concept of Maya

© 2021 David Churchill

All rights reserved. No part of this book may be reproduced or transmitted in any form or by any means, electronic or mechanical, without written permission from the author, except for the inclusion of brief quotations in a review.

Cover art: *Lily Evans* by Howard David Johnson
Interior artwork: "Tibetan Prayer Beads," Alison Chase Radcliffe
Book layout: Barbara Shaw

ISBN 978-0-9753095-8-2

First Edition

Published by:
Pony One Dog Press
Suite 113
1613 Harvard Street, NW
Washington, DC 20009

Contents

INTRODUCTION. A Textbook for Poets | xiii

CHAPTER ONE: An Interpretive Key | 3
    Holiday from Teaching | 5
    Alone with the Terrible Universe | 6
    Pleasure Dome | 7
    Driving to School | 8
    September, 2001 | 9
    Australian Merlot | 10
    Australian Shiraz | 11
    Reisterstown, October, 2001 | 12
    October Garden in Maryland | 13
    Bouviers | 14
    Solitude | 15
    November Morning | 16
    Another Evening, Possibly in December, as I Recall | 17
    Barbequing, Christmas, 2001 | 18
    Four Birds | 19
    March Afternoon | 20
    Friday, March 8, 2002 | 21
    April Dusk | 22
    October Dogs | 23
    April Birds | 24
    Poems in Progress | 25

CHAPTER TWO: Face of the Speaker | 29
    Return to Teaching | 30
    Dusk | 31
    Marrying Myths | 32
    A Storm Brewing | 34
    Palomino Leaves | 35
    My Companion and I Listen to Paco de Lucia Play *Solo Quiero Caminar* | 36
    November Love Poem | 37
    Love Poem | 38
    December, 2001 | 39
    House Finches | 40
    April Afternoon | 41
    Monday Evening | 42
    The Ant | 43
    After A Storm | 44
    Rattan Fans Circle the Ceiling | 45

CHAPTER THREE: The Revealing Power | 49
    The Frivolity of Language | 51
    The Stars | 52
    September Lament | 53
    Watching Two Squirrels | 54
    The Day After | 55
    Coral Voice | 56
    Ode to Ether | 57
    Gray April | 59
    Love Poem | 60
    Twilight | 61
    Bitten | 62

White Thursday | 64
Summer Love Poem | 65
Chilly Summer Dusk | 66
June Evening | 67
Here's to Writing a Poem on the 13th of Every Month for an Entire Year, but Knowing I'd Never Remember All That . . . | 69
Dark Matter | 70
Childhood | 72
A Rainy Thursday Afternoon | 74

CHAPTER FOUR: Theme Poems | 77
The Snow Leopard | 78
Himalaya | 79
Getting Hard To Tell | 80
Various Disguises | 82
Thoreau Says We Must Live Within Two Miles of Our Primary Childhood | 83
Baboons | 84
Wednesday | 85
The Ego | 86
Destiny | 87
Ode to Maple Seeds | 88
A Quick Look At Despair | 89
Rilke's Panther | 90
Grace of Gods | 91
Black Moon | 92
The Poem Lounges in a Chair, Late Morning | 94

Commentary on Select Poems | 97

Epilogue | 109

Acknowledgements | 110

About the Author | 111

Beware of Maya

–George Harrison

INTRODUCTION

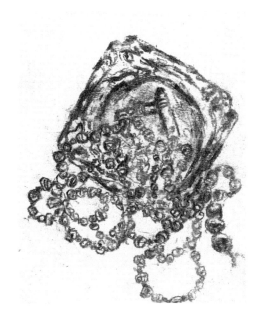

POETRY AND THE CONCEPT OF MAYA

A TEXTBOOK FOR POETS

WHEN I WAS AN ADOLESCENT, I carried a copy of *Stephane Mallarme, Poems*, translated by C. F. MacIntyre, wherever I went, in a specially-sewn inside coat pocket in a denim jacket. In addition to Mallarme's poems, the book contained an extensive section of NOTES, written by the translator as well as letters Mallarme had written about his poems and material from other sources. That, together with the poems themselves, was *my* textbook. This book follows the same format. Poems in several chapters, commentary at the end.

I would never however presume to write a "textbook" on any subject myself, let alone on poetry—except for one fact: this book is based on the poetry of Alan Britt, and *every* bookcase should house at least one—if not more—of Alan Britt's books.

His poems are canvases of impressionistic texture and detail that subdue the senses, even as they often leave our comprehension behind. Happily, however, his poems also possess a quality of *transparency*. But transparent not in the sense that his poems are obvious in their meanings, which they often are not, but in the sense of a device I like to call a "quizzing glass" (or to use a more recent analogy, like a pair of crystal spectacles), something to look through to bring things into focus, or to see more than one image of reality.

The idea that reality can have another, perhaps more real reality behind it suggested the possibility of approaching Britt's poetry from the point of view of the Hindu concept of *maya*. In Eastern religion, maya is the material world, that which hides the world of ultimate reality from us. This material world in which we live is also the world of lyric poetry. This could be one area where Eastern and Western philosophy possibly overlap. As maya encompasses the ephemeral, changing world of material images, lyric poetry concerns itself with our reactions to that world, to its shifting surfaces that envelope us.

Briefly then, the concept of maya is the belief that it's possible to see through the world of the senses to the permanent reality behind it. "Maya is the world of that rippling pond . . . " according to Joseph Campbell, writing in *Myths of Light*, "the fractured, sparkling image of reality that is no reality but only it's broken surface:"

> *Maya* is said to have three powers. The first power is called the obscuring power: it shuts out, as it were, the white light of eternity. *Maya* operates like a mask or curtain over truth.
>
> Or you might think of *maya* as a prism: the white light strikes the prism and is broken into myriad rays. This is the second, or projecting power. Here the forms of the world are projected, just as the light through the prism. The projecting power projects the world of broken forms
>
> The third power is said to be the revealing power, the power rendered in art, when through the forms we experience the radiance. When the radiance is experienced in art, the fascination of the art object is that of discovering your own true radiance there, because there is only one radiance, that is the radiance of full consciousness.

Lyric poems too have revealing power. "It is the function of art to serve / the revealing power of maya," according to Joseph Campbell. In this respect, Britt's poems are like those "quizzing glasses" I mentioned earlier, that were popular during the Regency Period. Though the former had only one lens, Britt's can have many. The symbols, metaphors and images deployed in a lyric poem—and we are only talking about lyric poems—are its lenses. It is through these that one looks in order to "quiz," to see what's going on behind the poem. These are the devices that make a poem transparent to its reality. Real-world maya too can be transparent. A beetle on a rose leaf, for example, could be the key to an existential truth; or the universe in a grain of sand.

POETRY AND THE CONCEPT OF MAYA

And just as there are some among us who can already look at the material world and perceive a spiritual dimension behind it, learning how to read, write and enjoy lyric poetry holds out the possibility to all of us, poets and readers alike, to see for ourselves how they do it, getting more enjoyment out of poetry in the process.

David Churchill
September 30th, 2020

CHAPTER ONE

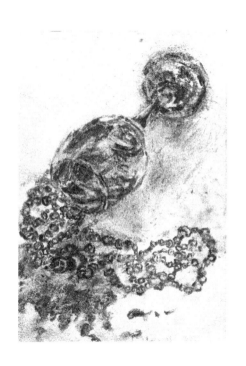

POETRY AND THE CONCEPT OF MAYA

An Interpretive Key

IN THIS CHAPTER you learn how to look through the lenses.

One way of looking through a poem's lenses is through the use of "interpretive keys." An interpretive key is something the reader brings from experience in his own life. By applying it to the world of the poem, meaning is unlocked. It is similar to a parable in the Old and New Testament. The purpose of a parable, according to Mark (Mark 4-12), is that "seeing they may see, and *not* perceive; and hearing they may hear, and *not* understand; lest . . . their sins should be forgiven them." (Italics mine.) God challenges those who come to him to study the messages and then to look into their hearts for the deeper meaning of his mysteries.

In other words, finding an interpretive key is the same as finding something in the poem to relate to. Start with what you relate to, and use that to illuminate other images in the poem. Take for example these lines of a poem called "Baboons"; after stating that baboons link man and dogs and that they bite their nails like stock market junkies, the speaker describes them as

> Staring into heaven
> with a no-vacancy sign around their necks.

Who is "staring into heaven," the baboons or the stock market junkies? Secondly, what does the "no-vacancy sign" imply? If you associate "no-vacancy" with motels, as I do, you immediately think of a place where there's no more room. And if you've ever stared into heaven, you might have found your head filling with thoughts like "why am I here" and "what is the meaning of life." Thus, by antithesis, the image of looking into heaven without room for any additional thoughts turns the conventional meaning of "vacant" on its head, no pun intended.

Try your hand on the selection of poems below. Always be mindful of how the action or sequence of a poem affects the relation of its images to each other. If you find one part that makes sense, see how many other parts you can fit with it.

Holiday from Teaching

Green castanets
spill over the sunken backs
of the horses of instruction.

So, today, these horses
reject their bureaucratic loads of hay,
reject their chrome blinders
riveted to harnesses of conventional wisdom.

Today, these sad horses,
almost as heavy as their precious enigmatic
tornadoes of jealousy,
arise
on weightless hooves
to look at the world
through the wild, clear eyes of joy!

Alone with the Terrible Universe

My shadow
attacks
the cedar
lattice
that surrounds
the patio.

Lamplight
flickering thick September maples
splotches
the muscular cedar boards.

A dog,
a small brown and white
dog barks
across a dark sea
of crickets
all hunched together
like millions of glistening coquina shells
on a black shore.

Pleasure Dome

That squirrel's nest, twenty-two feet above
my left shoulder,
tobacco-colored twigs and leaves
stacked high,
almost enough to fill
a small wheelbarrow.

This happens to be the perfect maple
for residence
since the main trunk lists
far to the right
creating a cool umbrella
of muscular green.

A gray and white cat
scampers through the damp waist
of late afternoon.

Echoes
of cars
paste
the sky.

Driving to School

On our neighborhood street
this fawn
faces me half a block away
then vaporizes down a drainage ditch
through misty predawn humidity.

As I pass by
a second fawn's slender whitetail
like a moonlit metronome
washes the drainage ditch's
wet grey concrete.

September, 2001

September has thick, emerald hair,
a thin waist of traffic,
and a distant white dog
gnawing the first hour of late afternoon.

September has seen buildings crumble,
grief worn like scarves.

The large body of October
already rises up
through yellow leaves
with tiny capillaries
slowed to a crawl
by a sudden Canadian chill.

September leans on a split-rail fence
and watches yellow leaves
sail by in a swirling gust of ashes.

Australian Merlot

The label says merlot,
but I swear it has that
wooden ambiance
more closely associated with cabernet.

Fire engines clot
our neighborhood street,
the fluttering artery
of the bourgeoisie.

Black dogs bark at the gate
as ashes of souls and asbestos
rain down on the neighborhoods.

Australian Shiraz

Fruit flies attempt to romance
this shapely, brunette shiraz.

She's tempting.

But, alas, the hand of fate
waves us all away.

So, I huddle
below early autumn fireflies
whose exhausted lime bodies
flicker momentary myths and naïve German fables.

Eventually, my severe gazes
send tracers of dotted green light
through night's tin roof
dusted by glistening, cocktail-lounge stars.

Nothing much to live for,
I suppose,
since fate has cultivated
more
than a casual infatuation
for my ruby-hipped,
bare-shouldered,
brunette shiraz.

Reisterstown, October, 2001

It's autumn dusk,
sunlight
a slab of butter.

This skin
of Friday afternoon,
chilly,
covered
with scales
sloughed
at fish markets
from Maine
to Maryland.

October Garden in Maryland

Green tomatoes
beg
to be left alone.

They droop,
talk in
whispers,
caress
each other's
hollow tubes.

Two golden tomatoes
in the back row,
translucent
large drops
of yellow
metamorphic
dozing tears.

A whitened wood stake
crippled
to the right.

Holding firm,
one orangered
beauty:
stark reality.

Bouviers

Our three herding dogs
tell the boys
on the other side
of a split-rail fence
it's high time
to reconsider
their annoying behavior.

As adolescent
yelling and banging
of maple sticks
against the cobblestone driveway
gradually subsides,
only the occasional bark
is required
to cultivate the herd.

Solitude

Wine's black hips slosh a pale, blood-stained carnation.

Napkins scattered like poker chips across the Formica
    table.

An ebony violin guides a blind and arthritic Peruvian
    jaguar
on a silken chain past our wheezy refrigerator.

November Morning

The coffee
steps out
of her Peruvian bean,
shivers
her mink feathers
in the cold.

The pink carnation,
humanity
disheveled to one side
of her face,
rouge
indiscriminately applied,
leans forward
like an exotic bird
or terrestrial saint,
a religion
of dried blood
like exhausted mascara
dusting the petals
above her eyes.

Another Evening, Possibly in December, as I Recall

An old black Bouvier staggers
up cement steps
covered
with worn artificial
green turf.

Above Shasta's grunts,
the iron railing
breathes a sigh
of rust and relief.

Yellow porch light.

A motorcycle,
abdomen
of bees,
cruises by
carrying the rare blue moon
in its side pouch.

Chrome studs
on the black sky
vibrate loose
as neighborhood dogs
splinter the icy darkness.

Barbequing, Christmas, 2001

The tongs,
bowlegged
like a Bolivian grandmother
shouldering clay jugs
from the river.

The propane tank
spattered
with psychedelic
rusted
free-roaming
tears.

Disintegrated, black grills
lean against
a carport brace,
sadly recalling
the glorious salmon
and squash days
of summer.

Four Birds

Raven, with a galvanized
washboard, glides above
a blue spruce.

Ford pick-up drags its disintegrated muffler,
lawn mowers, hedge clippers and rakes
slowly past our house.

Yellow finches flicker the jade pines.

Two female cardinals resemble
brass smoke rings.

Driftwood-colored warbler
shatters
the glass sky.

March Afternoon

An early afternoon mourning dove
devours a school bus
…an empty, yellow, woolly caterpillar
with black spots
behind its fuzzy head.

A male cardinal's
sharp whistles
sound like
raindrops
overflowing a galvanized bucket.

An orange cardinal,
smoky mask,
smoky shoulders,
sends spirals of mercury
around the bare arms
of a winter maple.

A siren pulses
a side street,
an aneurysm
in this otherwise pleasant
early March
afternoon,
as steady
Tai Chi light
coerces black diamonds
through the patio lattice.

Friday, March 8, 2002

A dried magnolia leaf
scuttles our carport
like a horseshoe crab.

Skittling her tiny points
of existence
across our chilly March patio.

But this magnolia leaf is already ancient,
several days ahead
of new buds
still bathing their beautiful roots
of amnesia
in utter darkness.

And, again, this
magnolia leaf
scuttles sideways,
tapping her jade fingernails
against the iridescent windows
of my thoughts.

April Dusk

Saber teeth
sunlight
splinter the lattice.

Long shadows,
slugs migrating the red torso
of silence.

Blue jays
cry
like flint.

Mockingbirds create
a chorus
of orchids
and switchblades.

October Dogs

Neighborhood dogs
wander across fences
with antler barks
and splintered howls.

Silver chains
slide from their shiny necks
into moonlit pools
of black water.

April Birds

A finch's neck
the color of rhubarb.

A sparrow taps
tin melancholy.

A goldfinch
warbles
then empties her pockets;
silver and bronze
foreign coins
cascade her feet.

Poems in Progress

You know, after abusing
these damn things,
some wounded, gashed, bleeding,
and holding their sides,
it's a wonder they trust me
at all to approach them,
considering their fragile conditions.

But I coax them,
time and time again,
urging them to reveal themselves,
cultivating generations
in their dark barrels,
knowing that any moment
could be my last.

CHAPTER TWO

Face of the Speaker

IN THE LAST CHAPTER we saw that though most of the action of the poems in this book seems to be confined to one suburban backyard, the psychic world of the speaker ranges back and forth in time and throughout the whole globe. Yet though we observed this by "seeing" through the poem's metaphors and imagery, we still recognize that a poem is more than a random collection of images. In this chapter we address the fact that the poem ultimately has only one unifying source, an author.

The idea is familiar from the parables in Scripture. In traditional Occidental theology, God is an "individual" with a distinct personality and set of traits. The individual as we understand it however does not exist in the Orient. They do not conceive of the individual as we do, as a self-actualizing free agent; in fact individuals hardly exist at all in the East except as they fulfill their roles in society. Their universe as a result does not even have a supreme being as a creator. No one watches what you do or judges you. It is all very mechanical.

Here's a subject for a paper: how do *haikus* compare with lyric poetry in this respect? Is it possible to perceive a person behind a *haiku*? We in the West want to see a face.

I suggest the best way to power up your quizzing glass is by asking how consistent the images are with each other. Do they share a consistent point of view? Are they narratively or logically related to each other? If a relationship is difficult to discern, ask if they at least resonate with each other? Are they like dream images? If all else fails, ask yourself this: is someone playing a trick on me?

Try your developing skills on the following poems.

Return to Teaching

Today I got to write
Federico García Lorca's name
on a green chalkboard!

So, the proof of my madness
is the dust on my fingertips
from a luna moth's struggling wings?

Anyway, today, I got to write
Federico García Lorca's name
on a green chalkboard!

Dusk

Silverblack tail twitches
on overhead
elephant branch.

Maple seeds helicopter
like copper finches
through my fading
green thoughts.

Marrying Myths

> *We want to put his ass in the stir!*
> *We want to pin this triple murder*
> *on him, he ain't no Gentleman Jim!*
>
> –Bob Dylan

I married a myth.
She drifted away.

I awoke
in the throat of a gold mine.

Hurricane Carter paid dearly
for his myth,
a myth spread by pallet knives
across the blemished forehead of Democracy,
a myth complicated by age-old extortion and bigotry.

But, tonight, I feel like dreaming
a new myth,
one with hips
of black wine,
one whose kisses resemble rainbirds
in shiny long black coats
strolling like stately gods of pepper
over St. Croix's windy white sand
strewn with bruised yellow
and green palm fronds.

A brand new myth,
one that takes the mystery
out of satellites
prowling much too high
above our clouds of freedom.

A Storm Brewing

This storm from the Great Lakes
thickens ink
that spurts
from my squid soul
as I dive
below the depths.

I drag ink across this paper:
feathered chameleon footprints
across Florida white sand
(as opposed to thick-ridged
government issue footsteps
on the lunar surface).

Half an hour later,
the wind cultivates deep arroyos
over my footsteps.

Then the storm
swoops down
like a sperm whale
several miles
below sunlight.

Cuts me in half
at the waist.

Palomino Leaves

Elements
crushed
by a red November wind:
twisted, wild
and curled
palomino leaves.

Dogs tapping
their opaque claws
upon these leaves
chilled by Canadian air
leave yellow footprints
in my blood.

My Companion and I Listen to Paco de Lucía Play *Solo Quiero Caminar*

The guitar note
bends
with ease
like a green thorn
beneath my bare foot.

Seeking my fatal flaw,
another guitar note,
a brittle thorn,
dives
through our entwined sensibilities.

A sinew
or a rusted
spring in your backbone
pulls away
from muscle.

I watch you
windblown
creak to and fro
like a whitewashed screen door
on a Georgia farmhouse porch.

November Love Poem

The harmonica is a young evangelist
just fallen
in love with a gypsy.

The gypsy is a garter snake
with hair and fingernails
of green fire
devouring large, festive dreams.

Each gypsy scale…a reed on the harmonica.

All colors, starting with bruised mango,
flow from the gypsy's hungry lips.

Blinded by love,
the harmonica
now recognizes the universe
as various colors:
assaulted amethyst, guava, and lemon sawgrasses
hidden
among the yellow sands
of despair.

Love Poem

I inhale the carnation,
her face
a hint
of intelligent rouge.

My shoulders
collapse
like old pigeon bones
upon the wire roost
of a tarpapered
tenement roof
in the Bronx.

December, 2001

Exhale more than you inhale.

Two or three times,
to make sure
you get it right.

Now swivel
your fountain
stool
in December's
black throat;
a month
of explosive neon
or arbitrary death?

Purple robes
refract
moonlight
that vaporizes
fingertips
on the flesh
of our
affordable gods.

House Finches

House finches, two of them,
have adopted
this ornamental porcelain
bird house
hanging by a thin chain
outside our back door.

She has the most gorgeous
coriander feathers,
eyes
two drops of black oil.

Her mate fluffs
his vermilion shoulders
of smoldering
coals.

It's late March,
early cardinals whistle
in loops
of water.

April Afternoon

Dog legs
flicker lattice;
Jacques' vermilion collar
alerts the aureole
orbiting
the robin's
dazzling green overture.

The robin
braids her song
around a thick gray maple branch.

Her song, a small garter snake
disguised as an asp
escaping
the golden cup
of truth.

Monday Evening

Maples hiss
when a May wind
rubs her hips
against their thick
green leaves.

Every bird in the neighborhood:
springs winding,
metaphysical pulleys in need
of religious oil,
melodic rivers
flowing past thin reeds,
all weightless
as Mozart flutes.

The Ant

Wind flares the ant's bronze tentacles.

Suddenly, the ant's glistening universe
struggles
with moments
of lost control.

This ant will experience many
such
moments
during his
short weeks of existence.

But today
he seems quite content
to roam
the blackened edge
of an old picnic board
lying on its stomach
in the thick ashes
of late spring mockingbirds.

After a Storm

Green smoke
licks the muscular ribs
of an algae-covered, split-rail fence.

Finches,
slashes of white
across their foreheads,
sharpen their
lexicons
against the feathery branches
of a giant blue spruce.

Humidity's
fingertips
warm the pulse
against my neck.

Rattan Fans Circle the Ceiling

Her Rococo smile
retains the
dissonance
of pampered violins.

Monsoon rain
darkens her linen shoulders
and glistens
the black street.

CHAPTER THREE

The Revealing Power

MY FIRST MEMORIES date from when I was around two: sitting alone in the back seat of an enormous car being driven over cobble-stones on an overcast day; the intensity of traffic lights: bluegreen, crimson, amber; the colors in a new box of crayons.

At that age things had an almost magical quality. No doubt it was because I was seeing everything for the first time, when everything had that halo of first-in-your-life newness. Today they are like embers under burned logs in a fireplace. From time to time I still see things I've never seen before, but now the heat is gone.

I believe the experience of being a two year-old corresponds most closely to the Eastern concept of *nirvana*. Earliest childhood is that time when all the conditions of nirvana are met, even to the point of not knowing you are in *nirvana*, for if you know you are there, as Joseph Campbell declares in his "Myth of Light" mentioned above, you are not there, for if the individual, ". . . beholding the divine, the divine landscape of the heavens with the holy sages and saints and all, if he so much as thinks, I have made it. I am here, this is my bliss, he goes right down the scale again, because ego has been enforced."

But for us in the West, ego *is* included, for we are above all else individuals, and once individuality is born in us, it becomes a permanent, immutable entity. Though in reality you may never be this body again, you will always be this individual who occupied a body. Once created, as Campbell says, "The ego concept is both expanded and annihilated, so that one's self is not identified with this temporal phenomenon here and now but the with reincarnating principle."

"Briefly," then, Campbell asks, "what is art in this view? Art is an arrangement of forms that will show that divine presence which is in all things through themselves. The radiance of art, the fascination of art, is the radiance and fascination of self-recognition in other; and that self is not the self of ego . . . but it is that inhabiting *atman-Brahman* that inhabits all things."

The poems we've been reading have that penetrating quality, the quality of things being seen for the first time. They recreate for us the delight of something new—and of experiencing for a moment the difficulty of not knowing what we're looking at until we've taken a moment to figure out what it is.

These poems are easier. Take your time with them.

The Frivolity of Language

The frivolity of language, sometimes
in the hands of a culture's most esteemed poets,
apologizes for its obscurity.

Until rains, like the seasons, wash away
raspberry and lime hopscotch poems
from weather-beaten sidewalks.

Damn, once again, hunkered in my basement,
staring at a child's plastic bucket filled
with squatty, pastel chunks of chalk!

The Stars

The stars are shamans.

They paint arroyos
the color
of Gilas:
bruised-orange,
black,
burnt-ochre.

Sand
flows through
the universe's thin waist,
emerges
from
cottonwood's
three hips
shaped
like
green
mantras.

September Lament

I'm trying to win the mind back,
snatching it from the jaws
of capitalist behavior.

Democracy was once a thirsty canoe
launched upon a philosophy of indigenous dreams
and wild rivers to nourish
the body of free society.

But now the white gloves of industry
are the ones spewing Maserati smoke
to obscure the scalping of entire nations.

I'm telling you,
despite chips falling
from the torso of a marble Venus,
there's a complex web
of imagination
expanding at an alarming rate
in the crawl spaces
of our split-level lives.

Watching Two Squirrels

Hips of wine
rest
above splotched yellowgreen
twisted
kneeling
bruised strawberry
and tobacco
colored
maple leaves.

The Day After

A woman's transparent eyes the color
of mantis eyes.

Pupils, tiny black seeds
at the center of pale jade.

Eyebrow twitches;
a flock of starlings sweeps sideways
as November exhales.

Dusk crosses her blue legs
nearby
in a white lawn chair.

Dusk doesn't say a word
as she glances across
the yellow eyelashes
of flowing broccoli.

Coral Voice

When you have the ocean,
a coral voice
sweeps you
beneath a handful of currents.

Though drowning in the temporal ocean,
still you're awash
in green and ivory
teeth and tongues.

But when you have the ocean,
you have plenty of time: weeks, months,
years, maybe, like a rhetorical pilgrimage of monks
across volcanic mountains of grief.

On the other hand, the coral voice
also resembles white sand,
that god, in his infinite wisdom,
has chosen to blow across your naked feet.

Ode to Ether

> *I hung my head.*
> *—Sting*

Sullen brown hair,
once a border
for Montana
blue eyes,
now tattered
by aluminum winds
crossing vast plains
enroute
to a neon cocktail glass
rocking
above
a Miami Beach nightclub.

Sullen brown hair
ripples and resembles
ultraviolet vibrations
on the black and gold
drone strings
of Sting's bass guitar.

Despair,
each feather
a bruised heartbeat.

Pour it
into a song,

or this poem.
Balance it
on the razored antlers
of brain cells,
if you prefer.

It'll etherize
into words,
anyway.

Gray April

So, I guess that's the danger
of moving too slowly.

Pretty soon, inertia.

A leopard slug
grazes on algae.

Black stones
rattle
a cardinal's beak.

Using zero as a reference.

Lime green
maple
embryos.

Love Poem

Crows wear loose-fitting attitudes
that fall like black tarps
over the spring order of things.

I've heard that lament before,
but like the horsefly
bugging heaven,
I confess
to ignorance
when it comes
to nagging questions of love.

New love,
like adolescent geometry,
dips its faith
into the pool of illusion.

Twilight

Robins announce darkness.

Punctuated by blue jay
on a rusted porch swing.

A manatee sheds its skin
and that's dusk.

Bitten

Once bitten by the brown recluse god,
you suffer
intensely.

You struggle,
but freedom
is a lock
whose key
lies hidden in a safe
guarded by the sales department
wearing long flowing robes
of black water.

Deacons, like waiters,
balance
collection plates
full of green salads:
fortunes,
or lies,
broadcast
across generations
of innocence.

The recluse god
appears
quite innocent
so as
not

to disturb
the harmony
of greedy bells
tolling the distance.

But, ultimately,
when you awaken,
you'll realize
you exist
merely as a finger
waving
at heaven.

After all,
whose life is it,
anyway?

In the end,
there is no assurance
that our souls
are woven from steel and orchids
or that some souls
are destined
to fly
like ragged strands of geese
across a winter landscape
of intelligence.

White Thursday

It's the air.

The skin of hippo or zebra
(whichever desires wet maples the most)
gurgles the gutters
of a White Thursday.

It's early summer.

A herd of purple crows
migrates
your eyelashes.

Your taut muscles
(as Mary Magdalene
rises up before you)
release
their linen robes
of absolute joy!

Summer Love Poem

I savor
the mockingbird's limp bag
of coins:
foreign metals
with alloys
rubbing smooth hips against copper.

Ribbons swirl
as an alchemist
braids the long silver hair
of summer dusk.

Venus
peers from behind the cattails,
then oozes
like a croc
beneath my green memory.

Chilly Summer Dusk

One hopes, of course,
that it's merely
a bit of cork
floating over the chilly waves
of my late afternoon chardonnay.

Who would've guessed
that embroidered plums
across your warm linen waist
could disturb the universe
or that tarantula rain could erase
everything from previous memory?

White wine,
on a particularly cool, summer evening,
softly stumbles into the room,
our room, motionless,
that now glistens
like a scarab
at dead midnight.

June Evening

You untangle
like an octopus
slow motion
in an earthquake.

The shower's coral tiles
glisten beaded tendons
against your neck
and mirror your irrational fears.

So, now,
I suppose fears, as long as they're old,
sometimes dry and crack
into corpses like those
on daytime TV dramas?

You were victorious once,
in a game that involved
jellyfish logic;
you believed the rustling
of thick, summer maples
would guide you
through the gates of hell
and into the beautiful claws

of yet another summer rain shower
tapping the
corrugated
tin roof
of love.

Here's to Writing a Poem on the 13th of Every Month for an Entire Year, but Knowing I'd Never Remember All That…

—For Carl Jung

Taboos are like bongos;
you find the beat
you like the most,
then discard the rest
in a pawn shop
on Greenmount Avenue,
hoping they'll materialize
into beautiful rivers
on a Baltimore Araber's ebony face.

Taboos were always meant to sprout black pearls
deep in the fertile souls
of humans.

All this elaborate masquerading of taboos
typically makes me hungry
and encourages my soul
to resemble a barracuda
trolling the dark shifting floor
of our mythical collective unconscious.

ALAN BRITT / DAVID CHURCHILL

Dark Matter

> *Understanding something you cannot see is difficult—but not impossible. Not surprisingly, astronomers currently study dark matter by its effects on the bright matter that we do observe. For instance, when we watch a nearby star wobbling predictably, we infer from calculations that a 'dark planet' orbits around it.*
> —Vera Rubin

The poet
sees dark matter at the bottom
of his wine glass.

Near the bottom of the glass,
he sees Magdalena's swirling waist of gravity
filled with the smoke of dark matter.

And Magdalena's eyes
of dark matter.

He knows all the vowels of bamboo that click
in a green wind blowing through Magdalena's voice
once grew in the thick, fertile soil of dark matter.

He touches Magdalena's hair,
flowing dark matter.

All the bassoons, oboes, and cellos
that orbit Magdalena's humid hips,
ah, create the irresistible pulse
of dark matter.

POETRY AND THE CONCEPT OF MAYA

The poet enjoys the last drops
of dark matter
rolling like sweat
down Magdalena's glass waist.

Childhood

For Rusty McClain

Hanging in the closets
of childhood
were secrets
followed by
embarrassments,
and small hand guns,
blue jays
of injustice
cocked
against cool darkness.

And just below the sweatshirt
not worn
in weeks
slept
the pearl-handled
egalitarian life
you were promised.

As anxiety
carved your
adolescent
grief,
each dawn
you arose

an outcast Phoenix
from the ashes
of your dreams.

A Rainy Thursday Afternoon

> *In raising a child, or a dog, discipline should never mean a withholding of love.*
> —Chanelle Britt

Chanelle thinks of this on our way
to the Y to deliver
Chelsea's forgotten membership card.

As we idle silver puddles,
the red
of a traffic light
ripples
their surface,
then a yellow
swallowtail
slowly migrates
a black puddle.

Until, finally, the green says,
I love you.
I've always loved you,
and always will.

CHAPTER FOUR

POETRY AND THE CONCEPT OF MAYA

Theme Poems

Many of the poems you've been reading so far, in true lyric fashion, are not about anything except themselves: a November evening, a bottle of wine, a difficult relationship, things in the speaker's immediate vicinity, in other words. Now we turn to poems that have a "theme." We are entering the realm of ideas.

Idea poems are often very straight-forward, but they can still deploy lyrical prosody. In this case, lyrical language usually performs three functions: it can reveal the meaning in a poem, expand the meaning or hide the meaning. Consider "Getting Hard To Tell," where a "bloody placenta / sprawled . . . " in the fifth stanza expands the meaning of the poem through an image of Christianity. In the last stanza, "one god-awful night, / my ghostly appaloosa and I," suggests a peyote experience undertaken as part of a Native American ritual.

By now you should be getting comfortable sensing on first glance—if not actually seeing—the existence of another layer behind Britt's "quizzing glasses." I say "another layer" rather than "meaning" because often another layer is only what you become aware of first, before you take that second glance. The second glance is when you begin to apply the skills you have been developing. That which is new takes more than a cursory glance to tell what it is. In deference to your developing skills, I will restrict my comments on the following poems in the discussion section, so find a friend who likes poetry too and share your impressions with him or her.

The Snow Leopard

Monks take their pilgrimage
through the ghostly dunes
of a snow leopard's fur.

Their capes flow like muscular lava
down steep crags.

The ibex is primarily Buddhist,
balancing all points of existence
on a jagged ledge.

The snow leopard digests the wisest part
of the blue sheep
in his long, elegant tail.

Himalaya

Ravens, vultures, eagles form an extended family
& greet one another with familial tension.

Bearded vultures shatter the tepid mountain
& devour the marrow
of a Buddhist mantra.

Blue footprints cross the forehead
of the Himalayas.

The snow leopard isn't water,
as much as we would like him to be,
but a nerve ending
orbiting, endlessly, orbiting.

Getting Hard To Tell

It's an eleven-hundred-dollar bottle
of Chilean merlot, or perhaps
Papa Joe's *Big Red*
signaling
from a buoy disguised
as a mermaid below the moonlit Atlantic.

I used to worship
the clouded berries
of your seaweed hair
before godmother invaded
my Brothers Grimm romance,
prowling my sheets and pillowcases.

I used to worship
uncanny freedom
until I stumbled
across guilt and despair,
not necessarily in that order.

Dressed as a male peacock,
shimmering for all he's worth,
I worshiped electric imagination.

And, sometimes, I even worshipped the Divine Providence
promised by a bloody placenta

sprawling like autumn across the granary floor
of a 19th century metaphor.

I worshipped it all!

Then rode like hell, one-got-awful night,
my ghostly appaloosa and I,
across the feral penumbra,
bleeding from our genocidal blue eyes.

Various Disguises

When you believe you've outsmarted death,
you inherit the most trouble.

Things appear out of the ordinary,
and that's just the beginning.

Phenomenology should clarify, but daily experience
proves as elusive as krill navigating
the baleen plates of a blue whale
rustling the southern coast off Sri Lanka.

Yet, existence mimics earthly possessions, too:
immaculate stereo speakers hand-built in Nashville,
Tennessee exhaling a muscular poetry more potent
than 19th century proselytizing composers
sentimentalizing their dimwitted youth
into a nationalist frenzy.

Unless you're a great blue whale from Newcastle,
Indiana, that is, heading straight for the Senior Special
at rush hour, just before the 50-millimeter Iraqi round
dissects your eldest grandson's liver into perfect fillets
of smoked salmon at a Vegas munitions tradeshow.

Ah, well, analogies don't exist anymore than
sentimental halters leading us to baptism, our daily
bucket of oats, providing us with religious shelter,
and all at the expense of the rancid truth
camouflaged in black and blue whale disguises.

Thoreau Says We Must Live Within Two Miles of Our Primary Childhood

I sleep.

Alarm clock's
green antlers
tear holes
in my significant dream
as solid as a wild mustang
of dry Arizona wind.

Raindrops splatter
like hollow, red,
shotgun cartridges.

Sleet hisses.

Baboons

Baboons link man & dog.

Biting their nails like stock market junkies

Staring into heaven
with a no-vacancy sign around their necks.

Dissolving hind claw behind right ear,
extracting things that need extracting.

Clouded leopard paints the mountain rocks
with a smoky presence outside midnight
mass near Cape Town.

One baboon, man-dog,
scans the shadows for intercourse,
a quickie, nightcap, perhaps,
one eye peeled for moonlit rocks
changing their spots.

Wednesday

The afternoon sun
drags her dirty-blond hair
across our kitchen table.

The late hour, a flock of starlings
blown like pepper
this way
and that.

November circles the house
in a burning red costume
designed to fool death.

The Ego

> *The ego simply disappears the moment you touch him.*
> —Kabir

Imagine diving
into daily existence
without intent
of finding something solid,
something rusted, perhaps,
but otherwise resembling an anchor,
say, from the *Wydah* or the *Santa Maria*?

My money's on the anchor, defending one
of the few sanctuaries we've got left.

And I'm not talking religion,
opiate to the masses,
although the ego must be stroked,
even during Midnight Mass.

The ego must be misunderstood like any good myth.

So, how do you caress the ego
without destroying it?
If Kabir had it all figured out
600 years ago,
how come we're still
dealing with this problem?

Destiny

Each poem has its feral destiny.

So, why interfere?

Intellectual leaps are obtained
through blind faith, anyway.

Or, we could continue slinging
fresh feces from behind the bars
of our miserable cages.

Ode to Maple Seeds

For Michelangelo Buonarroti

Maple seeds fall to the ground,
spiraling toward their heaven
that determines whether they survive and flourish
into full-grown maple trees
or disperse their atoms
for alternate purposes.

Same thing for humans,
only we float skyward
to our heaven,
which we'll never see
and never touch.

A Quick Look at Despair

Amidst all this debris
I have a life.

Such as it is or will be
at my age.

Amidst all the disappointments
that educated professionalism brings.

I fly in every direction!

My ultimate freedom
and despair.

Rilke's Panther

Freedom is a strange bird,
behind her guilty feathers.

Freedom is Maria
swaying to the lowest tango.

Maria harbors freedom
inside her ribcage,
freedom that perches
and paces
at oddest hours.

Blow up Maria's ribcage
with TNT, if you're a Loyalist.

But Immanentists
prefer another way.

Unlock the ribcage
with a modicum of grace or lust,
as you prefer,
but with deadly precision
separating the ribs
deliberately,
thus allowing freedom
to escape
the horrible suffering
of Rilke's panther.

Grace of Gods

It only appears primitive
because
traditional values
herd our youth
into
Burger Kings
and Pizza Huts
clogging their arteries
while they assume the position
of the ideal American family.

Flat teeth chewing cuds in Chicago
stockyards at frosty 4 AM
also endure innocence
while sadly awaiting
validation
for that nagging gloom
they cannot seem to elude,
a gloom which, tragically, includes
their ritual slaughter
of living
just outside
the grace of gods.

Black Moon

The black moon influences
our every waking moment.

We tried moving closer to the surface.

Straps that held our souls
were cinched tightly
via sterling tipped leather.

But circulation became hazardous.

Odd to develop breathing difficulties
with our faces motionless above the surface.

On either side of us
a hungry customer anticipating his daily salute
& a salesman with his hand on a shiny fender.

We eased backwards into the muddy river
like crocodiles.

Each carried the black moon
in his teeth like a delicate egg
to the silt & weeds
that lay at the bottom of misery.

Only it wasn't misery anymore.

Flames flickered like gold stripes
in our watery eyes.

Our rough skin began to glow in the darkness
as we gracefully wriggled
through our new opaque world.

Our claws were good
for scraping wet dirt & melancholy
nests for the new black moon
reproduced in each of our bodies.

I noticed my brother's teeth
were tusks that trailed fluorescent echoes
through the long, damp night.

The Poem Lounges in a Chair, Late Morning

The poem props its feet
upon a round, white table
loitered with colored pens & pastel paper.

Sunspots fall through dogwood branches
onto this poem.
The pattern resembles

the lumpy pad
of a dog's foot.
The poem changes

as a cloud thickens.
Three new cucumber flowers
emerge from the long hair of yesterday's storm.

Wild roses sway from the sleepy side
of our white house.
It's late May,

the late morning breeze has green eyes,
our neighbor's Carolina wrens
are at it again, dominating the conversation.

Across the road
a young German shepherd
behind a chain-link gate

challenges all walkers.
From our silver maple, the cardinal's song
is as clear as a blue river

flowering through an onion.
The outline of his notes
falls into a lawn chair shadow's Spanish guitar.

For a few moments the mowers fade,
the wasp floats like a lazy parachute
behind the head of a wild rose.

Mockingbirds, titmice & two brown headed cowbirds
discuss existential angels balanced upon iron stair railings
rusting along the bottom rung.

The heavy split rail fence curves
around the corner of the yard
before disappearing into a crowd of forsythia.

The sunspots have all but disappeared,
the sky mostly white
with various patches of swirled gray

as in Walt Whitman's beard
spread just above the trees.
It's nice having Walt visit

this poem, seeing as how he's the only
human being in it.
The sun grows its dog foot again.

COMMENTARY ON SELECT POEMS

COMMENTARY

Note: these comments are my own interpretations of the poems. They are given here only as illustrations of how at least one person reacted to them. Your interpretations will likely be different from mine, unique to your own experience in life. (Not all poems are discussed.)

CHAPTER ONE

Holiday from Teaching – What are the "horses of instruction?" Why would the speaker characterize crisp leaves as "Green castanets?" What time of the year is it? What could their "precious enigmatic tornadoes of jealousy" be?

Alone with the Terrible Universe – The first two stanzas of this poem are relatively straight-forward. What does the "black shore" suggest in the last stanza? Note the speaker's attitude: in medieval iconography, dogs are symbols of faith. The dog in this poem "barks / across a dark sea / of crickets . . ." Why crickets?

September, 2001 – What is this poem about? If September were a person, what would seem to be its attitude to what happened?

Australian Shiraz – One could make statements about many, if not all, of these poems that contradict each other yet could both be true at the same time. I believe this is true about this poem and that it was written this way on purpose. In other words, when you look at the bottle of shiraz, this quizzing glass shows two realities, one superimposed on the other, both valid at the same time. What could the two possible images for the bottle of shiraz be? The "naïve German fables" suggest the world of princes rescuing fair maidens, yet the speaker, far from being a prince, appears to be someone who hangs out in cocktail lounges. What single-word line relates these images? Is this poem ultimately very sad?

Reisterstown, October, 2001 – What is the weather on this Friday afternoon in October?

Bouviers – Another pretty straight-forward poem except for one word in the last line. What do you think the speaker means to imply about obedience with the use of this word?

Solitude – A short poem about the speaker's past. I infer this from the phrase "wheezy refrigerator," which suggests a repository of memories. Does the speaker appear in the poem? What kind of person do you think he used to be? What are some of his memories?

November Morning – Here's a poem about someone who loves coffee, especially on a winter morning! Coffee, like wine, is an elixir that brings troubling intrusions from foreign climates and places. What is the speaker's attitude and especially his or her vantage point on these intrusions from the past?

Another Evening, Possibly in December, as I Recall – What are the "Chrome studs" on a black sky? Why is a motorcycle an "abdomen of bees?" What is the "rare blue moon" in the motorcycle's side pouch?

Four Birds – This poem contains (at least) three sound images and two visual images. What are they? Which bird has the loudest call?

March Afternoon – Another not-so-simple simple poem. This poem paints sound images of four sounds. Also, as you may have come to expect in a Britt poem by now, the last stanza introduces a foreboding note into the otherwise quiet March afternoon. What is "Tai Chi"? Why does it suggest old people, trying to stay healthy?

April Dusk – Another seemingly simple poem. What comes to mind when you read the last stanza? Why does it seem to bring to mind the warring families of Montagues and Capulets from Romeo and Juliet?

April Birds – Another poem from Britt's aviary. Does anybody but me see characters from medieval guilds in these birds? Does the sparrow belong to a guild—or is he the town beggar, tapping his way down the street?

Poems in Progress – Who is the speaker in this poem—the poet—or you, the reader? If you construe "dark barrels" as wine barrels and ". . . generations / in their dark barrels," as alcoholics, is it possible the speaker is suggesting that either writing poetry or reading it could be a type of addiction?

CHAPTER TWO

Return to Teaching – Why does chalk-dust suggest moth wings to the speaker? Does this image seem consistent with the speaker's mood as he reveals it in the poem?

Marrying Myths – Here's a complicated poem. The fourth stanza contains one image that gives birth to six! To paraphrase the gist of the poem will hardly exhaust it's possibilities, so here goes: the speaker married his dream woman, they separated, he was left with a hoard of material for poems ("the throat of a gold mine"); the speaker then thinks of Hurricane Carter, a Black boxer who was wrongfully incarcerated; Hurricane's myth, I would argue, was to have a white girlfriend; perhaps a white girlfriend represented for him the epitome of what Democracy, unpacked ("a myth spread by pallet knives"), had to offer; for both however, the myth ultimately disappoints (Hurricane's perhaps landed him in jail); the speaker now wants a new myth, a woman of color (hips /

POETRY AND THE CONCEPT OF MAYA

of black wine), whose moist lips in their black lip-gloss ("rainbirds / in shiny long black coats") cover his body that already like the boxer's has been pummeled and bruised, in exciting kisses; the speaker then concludes with the hope that with this new woman his dreams will no longer be unobtainable. Given all this, what do you think the speaker's comparing himself Hurricane Carter tells us about his mood?

A Storm Brewing – This interesting poem opens with a powerful image of the speaker diving for safety into the depths, and ends with the storm swooping down after him like a sperm whale. In-between this extended metaphor, the speaker characterizes his writing, that has been inspired by the approach of the storm, as a series of footprints. What can you gather from the images in this section? Do they describe the act of writing, or the subject?

Palomino Leaves – Why are the yellow leaves in this scene described as "Palomino" leaves? Is it because of their color, or the way they look like a herd of wild horses when the wind sets them blowing? What does the speaker tell us about himself through his linking of "a *red* November wind" with "yellow footprints / in my *blood*"?

November Love Poem – This is a simple yet effective poem that describes the effects of a gypsy on a young religious man. The second stanza is the best description of a Flamenco dancer in motion I have ever read.

House Finches – In this subtle poem, the speaker describes two finches setting up housekeeping in an ornamental bird-house. Stanzas two and three, descriptions of the pair, are couched in domestic terms (coriander, oil, coals). What is the speaker's reaction to this setting up of their housekeeping? Is there anything in the poem that would indicate the speaker has any doubts about it? Do the whistles of the cardinals seem to sound a warning note?

Monday Evening – Here is a delightful yet at first glance confusing poem. It seems to picture the advent of one season in conflict with the season it is replacing. The image of birds winding their springs, that are then likened to "metaphysical pulleys," is captivating. The fact that the whole scene is then accompanied by orchestral music only deepens the mystery.

After A Storm – Here's another poem where, as in *Dusk* and *Palomino Leaves*, the speaker describes a scene in his first stanzas, then records his impression in the last stanza. Is the speaker's reaction in this poem in accordance with the scene he describes?

Rattan Fans Circle the Ceiling – This brief poem suggests another way to read Britt's shorter lyrics as a series of *haikus*. The first stanza (or *haiku*) in this poem presents the image of a woman in terms of a cloying excess. This is intensified by an almost violent excess of rain outside in the second stanza (or *haiku*). This is a good example of the way in many of Britt's lyric poems where the speaker describes a single scene that has caught his attention, very much like a photograph in words. Here the image of the woman is effaced in the second stanza, while the image we are left with, the image of the street outside, comes forward. What can you say about this final interplay of shadows?

CHAPTER THREE

The Frivolity of Language – This is a poem in which the poet steps forward and speaks in his own voice. Do you feel you already know him? Note the poem seems to contain no "lyric" or "quizzing glass" images. The image of the "hopscotch" poems and the "pastel chunks of chalk" seem to refer only to themselves, grounded in the world of maya. But are they really?

The Stars – A comment on the span of a human life compared to the eons of the stars. "Arroyos" are shadows across the ground but why are they compared to "Gilas?" Why does the poem end on the word "mantras?" Does the speaker feel he must recite mantras in order to walk safely through this landscape, to withstand its spiritual immensity as he traverses it?

September Lament – This is a pretty poem. After a to-the-point beginning, two-hundred-and fifty years of American history are summed up in two stanzas. All that's left of the ideals of Democracy are relegated to the last stanza. What does the speaker mean by our "split-level lives?"

Watching Two Squirrels – What could the "Hips of wine" be in this poem? Why is the poem titled "Watching Two Squirrels?"

The Day After – What is this the "Day After" of? Notice how the speaker injects a note of tension through his description of the first woman's eyes. How do the two women relate to each other? Does it seem they have made up with each other since the day before? Beyond the drama of the women, notice how the speaker manages to characterize the experience of a November dusk through their interaction. This is a fine example of a poem conjuring deep meteorological effects through the subtlest of dramatic details.

Coral Voice – What is a "Coral Voice"? What does the speaker tell you about the two types of ocean in the poem?

Ode to Ether – This poem, which I take to be an ode to a young woman who ended up a topless dancer (or a cocktail waitress) in Miami Beach, remind me that in interpreting a poem, it is the reader who brings order to the poem, not the poem that orders the reader's interpretation. Just so, I suspect, maya is a product of our own minds, and in learning to see through maya, we are actually seeing deeper into ourselves. I take "now tattered / by aluminum winds / crossing vast plains" as a clue to the cause of the young woman's downward spiral. The words "aluminum winds" conjure cars and mobile homes speeding down a highway. Note that "ether" has two meanings. Does the speaker deploy both of them?

Twilight – Here's a poem that manages to be striking in all of only five lines! Are the blue jays really on a rusted porch swing, or is that an image of the "noise" they're making? What is the impact of the last two lines? First we're in someone's back yard, then we're under water somewhere in Florida. The image of the manatee suggests to me the subconscious, beginning to stir.

Bitten – I take this as a poem about the pain of being a poet (or some other creative). Notice how the frustrations and disappointments of the creative's life are depicted in the poem's tapestry of images.

Summer Love Poem – This speaker's impressions of the call of a bird and the feel of a summer dusk need no comment, but I can't pass up calling attention to the image of Venus sinking behind the cattails like a crocodile. Does the first stanza suggest the "love" in this poem is somehow being paid for? How does the image of Venus going down expand on this?

June Evening – A failed relationship. Notice how much detail about the relationship and where it went wrong the speaker is able to convey through the images.

Childhood – The topic of this poem should be pretty obvious in today's world. What images suggest what the friend's "secret" is? How do you think the speaker feels about the subject of the poem?

A Rainy Thursday Afternoon – Notice how the speaker describes the traffic signals. The first is red, the last green, the second is "a yellow / swallowtail" crossing a black puddle. Why is this different from the other traffic lights? Do you think the "Chanelle" the poem is dedicated to might have been wearing a yellow raincoat?

CHAPTER FOUR

The Snow Leopard – This is a densely meaningful poem. I believe it all hinges on what meaning you give to the snow leopard. It seems clear the snow leopard is more than a real animal. It is obviously also an image of the world of the Buddhist monks. Does anyone agree the "ghostly dunes" of the snow leopard's fur are snow drifts? The "blue sheep" being digested in the snow leopard's tail remind me of westerner philosophers, cold in the harsh environment, who have come to learn from the monks.

Various Disguises – What does the "blue whale" symbolize? Notice how the speaker deploys the lyrical turn whenever the whale appears. Notice too how the whale appears first in a simile then in its own right as a symbol. Did you get the feeling, as I did when I read the last line, that "everything is death"?

Wednesday – They say the best still-life paintings, among their cornucopias of fruit and swags of floral opulence always contain some subtle reminder of the transitoriness of life: a bruise on a piece of fruit, a broken-off sprig of leaves, a fly . . . Have you begun to notice how many of these poems that make you see the ordinary with fresh eyes—are about death? Have you also noticed how often the color red appears in conjunction with the winter and the month of November; as in the "red November wind" of *Palomino Leaves*, the "red shotgun shells" of *Thoreau Says We Must Live Within Two Miles of Our Primary Childhood* and here in the "burning red costume / designed to fool death." Why would one naturally associate red with the gray of winter?

Rilke's Panther – Immediately look up a copy of *The Panther* by Rainer Maria Rilke. What is it that "core / in which a mightily will is standing stunned"? Now turn back to Britt's poem and as yourself, what is the "lowest tango" that Maria sways to? After all these years I finally realize what it is that is being stifled in the panther in its cage—and how powerful that drive is, that can destroy an image in its heart! Also notice how Maria's ribcage mirrors the cage of the panther, as well as a too-tight corset.

Black Moon – This fascinating poem stumped me. I immediately turned to the internet where I found this:

> The [black moon] is a second new moon that occurs during one calendrical month. Some believe [a black] moon will pull out our darkest feelings, our scariest skeletons, everything we keep hidden and would rather continue to avoid. It's a time that drama might ensue, for all the negative emotions of the spectrum, like envy, hatred, and revenge, will sit at the surface of everything. However, they have to be released sometime, and the black moon is here to help with the purging process, dragging your deepest strengths and desires to the forefront, uninhibited. (From *Elite Daily* Feb. 2, 2018)

But this is not the meaning of the black moon in this poem. An astrological black moon is a moon that purges all that is negative in us (as indeed it must be released sometime). It is a revealing moon. The black moon of the poem is different. Let's take it in stages: night, time of dreams and spirits; the moon, the light of the night; black moon, the darkness of the night, the night of the night. Thus the black moon symbolizes the cloaking or hiding power of the night, especially the fecund secrecy of the dark, the Jungian essence of the night itself. It clearly does not refer to the astrological black moon, quoted above, whose meaning is almost opposite.

So what do the images of the amphibious animals, for whom the demands of ordinary life appear to be suffocating, signify? Stanza six, beginning "On either side of us," describes a couple of scenes in ordinary life, so it seems clear where we are located. The lines in stanza twelve, ". . . for the new black moon/ that reproduced in each of our bodies," seem to indicate that the black moon, whether it be a sleep deeper than sleep, or a mystic intensity of dreams—or the renewal power of death itself; whatever it is, it evokes a positive transformation in the animals, making this a poem that is easy to understand but difficult to interpret.

The Poem Lounges in a Chair, Late Morning – I included this extended metaphor for a poem for one reason only; though it is full of eidetic images and secondary metaphors worthy of being mentioned on their own. The middle of stanza eight contains one of the synesthetic images Britt uses through-out his poems, that I may not have brought to your attention before. This one reads:

> . . . . the cardinal's song
> is as clear as a blue river
>
> flowing through an onion.

A birdsong as "clear as a blue river" seems easy enough to get, but what of the "onion?" Why is the river flowing through an onion—unless the onion is another "synesthetic" image, this one for the sky, a sky that is grayish white, and that has the feel of something sharp, crisp and aromatic-tasting—almost tear-inducing? As a side note, what effect do you think is created by describing the sun falling through the leaves overhead as casting the shadow of a dog's paw on the poem, a paw that seems to be in motion?

EPILOGUE

To look at life with a poet's eye is to have double vision—to see the world before you in all its beautiful and perplexing variety—and to see another image of it, a double of itself, the reality behind the reality, an effect not of a blow to the head or of being cross-eyed, but of the world itself. Training to be a poet could be training to be a saint—or a madman.

Alan Britt comes closer to this in his poetry than any other poet I know. I would like to have his freedom and assurance in my writing, but I can't do it. I would like to say with Britt that the sky "is an onion" or a piece of soap, but the most I can manage is "rosebuds pushing through their green foreskins" or, about tress in the fall, "still-bursts of autumn," images that remain firmly tethered to their referents.

Maya is too much in me. In fact, I am all maya. I have already struggled and lost. I never succeeded as a young man in following the footsteps of Arthur Rimbaud in "disordering my senses." Logic and order are the languages of maya. They are what hold the universe together. Strive as I might to imitate Britt, I can't get over the fear of going beyond it. I'm afraid of not being understood. I'm afraid of losing touch with what reality I do have. I already feel people beginning to turn away from me. I fear I may end up speaking gibberish on street-corners.

So I will buy a new coat and sew a new pocket inside to carry this book with me. This—or any other book by Alan Britt—will be my new textbook. I will take his book and whenever I start feeling constrained and overdetermined in my writing, longing to throw off the confines of reason, I will consult it the way writers consult dictionaries—or maybe I'll just hold it, the way some people hold Bibles.

ACKNOWLEDGEMENTS

ALL POEMS with the exception of the following appeared in *Alone With the Terrible Universe* by CypressBooks, Rio Rico, Arizona, 2011, The Frivolity of Language, The Ego, Destiny, A Quick Look at Despair, Getting Hard to Tell and Various Disguises appeared in *Lost Among the Hours* published by Rain Mountain Press, New York City, 2014; Baboons published in *Alan Britt, Greatest Hits 1969-2010 (and beyond)*, Pudding House Press 2020; Ode to Maple Seeds appeared in *Parabola Dreams* by Alan Britt together with Silvia Scheibli, published by Bitter Oleander Press, 2013; Rilke's Panther and Grace of Gods were published in *Gunpowder for Single-ball Poems* by Concrete Mist Press, 2020; Black Moon and The Poem Lounges in a Chair, Late Morning was published in *Infinite Days* by the Bitter Oleander Press, 2003

ABOUT THE AUTHOR

Alan Britt has published 18 books of poetry, his most recent being *Gunpowder for Single-ball Poems* (2020); *Ode to Nothing* (English/Hungarian–2018); *Lost Among the Hours* (2015); *Violin Smoke* (English/Hungarian–2015); *Alone with the Terrible Universe* (2011); *Greatest* Hits (2010); *Hurricane* (2010); *Vegetable Love* (2009); *Vermilion* (2006); *Infinite Days* (2003); *Amnesia Tango* (1998); and *Bodies of Lightning* (1995), plus the anthologies (selected): *The Music of the Aztecs: Poets of the DC Magic Theater Poetry Club*, Pony One Dog Press, Bethesda, MD (2019); *Concrete Mist Anthology*, Concrete Mist Press, York, PA (2019); *Black Lives Have Always Mattered: Essays, Poems and Personal Narratives*, 2Leaf Press, New York (2017); *Resist Much/Obey Little*, Spuyten Duyvil Press, New York (2017); *Nuclear Impact: Broken Atoms in Our Hands*, Shabda Press, Pasadena, CA (2016); *Alianza: 5 U.S. Poets in Ecuador*, CypressBooks, Rio Rico, CA (2015); *The Poet's Cookbook: 33 American Poets* with German Translations, Forest Woods Media Productions/Goethe Institute, Washington, DC (2010); *American Poets Against the War*, Metropolitan Arts Press, Ltd., Chicago/Athens/Dublin (2009); *Vapor transatlántico (Transatlantic Steamer)*, bilingual anthology of Latin American and North American Poets, Hofstra University Press/Fondo de Cultura Económica de Mexico/Universidad Nacional Mayor de San Marcos de Peru, New York and Peru (2008); *La Adelfa Amargo: Seis Poetas Norteamericanos de Hoy*, Ediciones El Santo Oficio, Peru (2003); *Fathers: Poems About Fathers*, St. Martin's Press, New York (1998); *From the Hudson to the World: Voices of the River*, Pete Seeger's Hudson River Sloop Clearwater Press, Peekskill, NY (1978); *For Neruda, For Chile*, Beacon Press, Boston, MA (1975); and *The Living Underground*, Whitston Publishers, New York (1973).

His 2013 Library of Congress interview with Grace Cavalieri for *The Poet and the Poem* is available on the LOC website. ABC Radio National (Australian Broadcasting Corporation) in July, 2008, broadcasted a straight read, plus live stream on their website of Alan's poem, "After Spending All Day at the National Gallery," as part of their Poets on Painters series.

Alan received his Master's Degree from the Writing Seminars at Johns Hopkins University. He teaches English/Creative Writing at Towson University and lives in Reisterstown, Maryland, with his wife, three dogs and one cat.

NOTES

CPSIA information can be obtained
at www.ICGtesting.com
Printed in the USA
JSHW051916120221
11882JS00003B/14